Childhood Hills

For Ken Bruen

*Ken,
Warmest regards,
Pat
April 18, 2002*

Childhood Hills

by
Pat Mullan

Writers Club Press
San Jose New York Lincoln Shanghai

Childhood Hills

Copyright © 2000 by Pat Mullan

This book may not be reproduced or distributed, in whole or in part, in print or by any other means without the written permission of the author.

ISBN: 0-595-09307-8

Published by Writers Club Press, an imprint of iUniverse.com, Inc.

For information address:
iUniverse.com, Inc.
620 North 48th Street
Suite 201
Lincoln, NE 68504-3467
www.iuniverse.com

URL: http://www.writersclub.com

For Annemarie,

Sean,

Maureen,

Brian,

Caomhe

and Caitlin.

Contents

Letter from Pat Mullan ---------------------------------------ix
In the Beginning ---xvii
The Poetry --1
The Early Years ---3
    Childhood Hills --3
    Craw ---5
    Craw: 1944 ---6
    The Lie --7
    The Quarry Hole --9
    Against the Blue Sky ----------------------------------11
    We Never Talked ---------------------------------------14
    Sundays ---15
    Enslaved --17
    Soul Food ---19
    Bicycle Ride --20
    The Champions ---21
    Uncle Peter ---23
    The Bird --26
    Small Victory ---28
    Paddington Station ------------------------------------29
The Later Years --31
    Paris ---31
    The Dancer --33
    The Turning Point -------------------------------------34
    April Sixteenth ---------------------------------------35
    Hampton Sunset --36
    The Gamble --37
    For Seamus Heaney -------------------------------------38

Childhood Hills

The Town I Love so Well… — 39
- Uijongbu — 45
- The Elevator — 46
- The Bank — 47
- Exoggle — 48
- Looking for Hemingway — 50
- Edinburgh — 52
- The Elegant Crane — 53
- Conversations with Caitlin — 54
- Leaving — 55
- Granny Bunty's Button Box — 56
- Savages — 58
- You always Wondered — 61
- On the Way to Connemara — 64

Introducing Annemarie Mullan Whilton — 65
- My Cat — 67
- Eyes — 68
- Grass — 69
- Storm — 70
- Obituary — 71
- Monday Morning — 73
- Your First Day at Dollys — 74
- My Dad is Home — 75

In Memoriam: James Dickey — 77
About James Dickey — 79
James Dickey's Poetry: The Religious Dimension — 81
Bibliography — 97
**And, Finally: © Of Conscious Evil and
©Who Killed Hammarskjold?** — 99
- Extract from the novel © Of Conscious Evil — 99
- Extract from the novel ©Who Killed Hammarskjold? — 103

About the author — 121

Letter from Pat Mullan

Connemara,
Ireland.
October 11, 1999

Dear Reader:

Let me tell you a little about myself. I was born in Ireland but I have lived much of my life in the United States of America. Six years ago I left a senior position in finance in the US and returned to live in Connemara in the west of Ireland. I had always wanted to write but I had never had the time. Of course, that was a convenient excuse. I was afraid that, if I ever sat down to write, I'd discover that I couldn't. I never wanted to find that out. So my busy life protected me. Until I took the plunge and came to live here in Connemara. I have always read different kinds of books but the thriller novel has been my favorite form of escapism. I often thought I could write one myself.

Four years ago, I forced myself to write. I reserved three or four hours each day for writing. In those early days I only wrote using pen and paper. I would type it later into my computer. The word processor was the most efficient way to revise and cut and paste. But there was something distinct about the symbiosis between my hand, the pen, the paper and my mind; something that harnessed my creative mind, something that was missing when I used the computer keyboard. The weeks and months passed and one page turned into ten and ten into fifty. Soon I realized that I had written 25,000 words of my first novel and that I had created a family of characters. The new world they inhabited took over my consciousness. I stayed with it. It's a lonely pursuit and one that demands lots of fortitude and stamina. Those virtues are probably as important, if not more so, than the basic ability to write. I finished that novel, © *Of Conscious Evil*, and it will soon be published in paperback in the UK. You will be able to get it, via the Internet, on *Amazon.co.uk*; I have completed about 85,000 words of a new novel, *Who Killed*

Childhood Hills

Hammarskjold?, and I have another 15,000 words to find. I have included a chapter from each novel at the end of this book. I borrowed that idea from James Patterson whose thriller novels I find addictive. His publisher cleverly adds a couple of chapters of his next book at the end. To whet the appetite. I have done the same thing here with *Of Conscious Evil* and *Who Killed Hammarskjold?*

So the muse was always there with me. But I exorcised it by scribbling poems that conveyed my feelings or described an event I had witnessed. Over the years this became a kind of poetic diary. I never considered myself a poet. I still don't. When I think of poets I think of names like Yeats or Wordsworth or Seamus Heaney. Seamus and I boarded together at St. Columb's College in Derry. In those years there was no sign that Seamus would one day become a Nobel Prize winning poet. When I think of American poets I think of Theodore Roethke, Galway Kinnell, W.S.Merwin, John Ashberry, James Dickey (of whom I will say more later), and Dan Masterson who once told me "you can write—no doubt about it…you have a voice that is your own and that's important. I want to help your voice confine itself to the pure statement that carries the image to the reader."….

I get most enjoyment from listening to a poet talk about the written work and the work in progress: why a poem was written, the spark that ignited the vision, the snatch of overheard conversation, the incident that retrieves a past memory, the choice of words and imagery, the simple scene transformed, the need to be a witness. I don't think that any of my poems need such an introduction. My work is simple, accessible, and unencumbered with intellectual reference; you won't need a degree in English literature to enable you to comprehend it. Nevertheless, I feel that a brief guide might add some value. *The Early Years* are exactly that: vignettes of life growing up in Derry in Northern Ireland with some searing memories of the subliminal fear imposed by the political, religious and educational systems. *The Later Years* are a collection of those scribbled poems that form that 'poetic diary' that I spoke of earlier. Speaking

Pat Mullan

of the 'spark that ignites the vision', a photo that I took of an old man in a rice paddy in Korea was indeed the spark for the poem *Uijongbu*. I was in the US army in Korea and we were out on a march through the countryside when we passed that old man working in his rice paddy. He looked at me, the exact look that I still see in the photo, and that was the 'spark'. My love poems need only one comment which I am borrowing from the Irish poet Michael Longley; speaking recently at a poetry reading at the Clifden Arts Festival (here in Connemara), Michael said "…for me I'm not alive as a writer unless I write a love poem…."

Is a writer born or is a writer made? I don't believe that question has ever been satisfactorily answered. I always knew that I wanted to paint (yes, I try to find time for my art when I'm not writing) and that I always found it easy to write. My daughter, Annemarie, seems to have inherited the same gifts. She has always been able to draw and from her earliest years she could write. So I have included a few of the poems she wrote when she was only fifteen. I think you'll agree that she has her own voice too and that, even at fifteen, she understood how to use the poet's tools of personification and metaphor. I have also added a couple of her more recent works. In these you can see a different voice, one 'sparked' by the visions of her life today.

When putting this small collection of mine together I realized that it would not be complete without talking about James Dickey, a poet who raised my consciousness at a time when I was not writing any more, a time when I had abandoned it, a time when the muse had departed. Well, James Dickey has now departed. He died on January 19, 1997. I suppose he was best known for his novel *Deliverance* but he also wrote about 20 volumes of poetry. *James Dickey's Poetry: The Religious Dimension* is my elegy to the man.

Sincerely yours,
Pat Mullan.

In the Beginning

In the Beginning

I was born in County Derry, Northern Ireland. Derry derives from the Gaelic/Irish word *Doire* meaning 'oak grove'. Oak groves were sacred places for the Celts. 'Oak' placenames can be found throughout the continent of Europe, including Britain and Ireland. St. Colmcille (also known as St. Columba), credited as the founder of Derry, established a monastery there in the sixth century. He was a prince of the great O'Neill family and the monastery was a gift from his cousin, the Prince of Aileach. He later left Ireland to establish his monastery on the Scottish Island of Iona and commence his mission to spread his Celtic Christian church.

Throughout the second half of the sixteenth century, Queen Elizabeth I of England tried to conquer the province of Ulster, the only part of Ireland that remained outside English control. The English first came to Derry in 1566 but the garrison established there at that time lasted only a few years. A second, more successful garrison returned in 1600 during the 'Nine Years War' against the Gaelic O'Neill and O'Donnell earls. The O'Neill and O'Donnell chieftains were defeated and they and their supporters fled to the continent ('Flight of the Earls'). Gaelic Ulster was left leaderless. James I, the new king in England, decided on a plan that would guarantee that Ulster would be subordinate to the Crown of England. He colonized Ulster ('Plantation of Ulster') with loyal English and Scottish settlers who were Protestant, unlike the Catholic Irish. The county of Derry was granted to the wealthy trades' guilds of London and the city was renamed Londonderry in honor of this association.

Childhood Hills

This was the legacy that I inherited as my birthright. I was born into a Catholic family but one branch of my family was Presbyterian. My great grandfather, Thornton Mullan, is buried in the graveyard of the Presbyterian church in the village of Eglinton in County Derry. When I was eleven I started secondary school at St. Columb's College in Derry. The school was run by priests who were armed with leather straps to exact physical punishment for any infringement of the rules or for any failure in class. Its ideology was conservative Catholicism. My generation in Derry at that time were beginning to question the right of the church to dictate their lives and the right of the British northern state to treat them as disenfranchised second class citizens. These stirrings led to the civil rights marches of the sixties and to the eventual revolution on the streets of Derry and Belfast, a state of affairs still unsettled. Some of my classmates are household names: Nobel Prize winning poet Seamus Heaney, composer Phil Coulter, writer and journalist Eamonn McCann.

As I write this today on this 11th of October 1999, Senator George Mitchell is back in Northern Ireland conducting his review of the failing *Good Friday Agreement* which he worked so hard to achieve.

For another look into this past of mine here is an excerpt from my novel *Of Conscious Evil*:

> At eight the next morning, Owen and Kate drove through the gates of Ardree House and headed north. It was a six hour drive to Derry, their first destination. Derry was Northern Ireland's second city. The city lay just north of the border that separated the British governed Northern Ireland from the independent Republic of Ireland. They planned to drive north through counties Sligo and Donegal. No rain was forecast. This was Kate's first time in Ireland and she looked forward to the journey.

Owen lapsed into silence as they got closer to Derry; Londonderry to those who considered themselves British. But it was always Derry to MacDara. He had a love-hate relationship with the place. He'd won a scholarship to St. Columb's College when he was eleven and spent four years there as a boarding student. St. Columb's was run by priests although half the teachers were lay . It was there that MacDara's reverence for priests and awe for the institution they represented had ended. Maybe it was there that the seeds of agnosticism, or even atheism, had been sown. MacDara preferred to think of himself as a secular humanist these days. Eccentric priests had dominated the classrooms. Father Toner, who taught mathematics, would often pick up the heavy bound Hall's algebra and whack an unsuspecting student across the side of the head. MacDara remembered one of many incidents.

"MacDara, where's Doolan today?"

Father Toner purposely mispronounced Dolan's name. Dolan was not a boarder. He was a day boy and lived at home in the city.

"He's sick, Father."

"How do you know that, MacDara?"

"Well, he said he wasn't feeling well in class yesterday, Father. So I assumed he was sick today."

"You assumed, MacDara! You have no proof!"

"No, Father."

"Q.E.D., quod erat demonstrandum. Proof, MacDara! In other words, you don't know and you lied to me."

"Isn't that correct, MacDara?"

"No, Father!"

"I said, isn't that correct, MacDara?"

"Yes, Father."

"Come up here!"

MacDara could still feel the sting in the palm of his hands from the six slaps that he received for lying from the leather strap that always hung threateningly just inside the side pocket of Father Toner's long, dark

Childhood Hills

soutane. St. Columb's was Catholic to the core. Its original role had been to prepare boys for the priesthood and that was still a principal mission. The church controlled the education system. Newspapers and radios were banned at the College. Outside influences and distractions were to be avoided at all costs. All evidence of civil authority was absent. The authority of the Church was paramount. Small rebellions preserved the sanity of the few who refused to become brainwashed by the system. MacDara was one of those few. They used to draw lots to choose a volunteer who would risk scaling the high walls that surrounded the grounds and making it to Wee Johnny's in Bishop Street to buy a packet of Woodbine cigarettes, the cheapest available. They had a special hideout behind the walls where they smoked while someone kept a lookout for the prefects. They also made radio receivers, crystal sets they called them, MacDara recalled. He remembered the night that the Dean had entered his dormitory after lights out and tripped over a crystal set earthing wire he had tied to the metal leg of the adjoining bed. That got him twelve, six on each hand with a leather strap, outside the Dean's office the next morning. His hands had swollen to double their size after that; couldn't hold a pencil in class that day.

His reverie was broken by Kate.

"Where are we now"?

Looking around, MacDara could see that they had entered the Strand Road and were heading uptown towards the Guildhall and Shipquay Street, a very steep street that led up to the Diamond, the center of Derry's shopping district. A British war memorial dominated the center of the Diamond. The Bogside lay on the low flatland beyond the Diamond, land outside the walls of the City, land where the poor and the powerless lived. The Bogside was fertile breeding ground for militant Irish republicans. It was the center of Civil Rights rebellion and protest against the British authorities in the sixties and seventies. One of the most photographed gables of a house in the Bogside still proclaimed 'You are now entering Free Derry.'

Once again, MacDara's reverie was broken by Kate.

"Owen, where are you? What are you thinking about?"

Pat Mullan

"Oh, nothing deep, believe me", MacDara lied, "just an old tongue twister; say this quickly: 'Shipquay Street's a slippy street to slide upon.'"

"I think you've regressed to your childhood. Is that what this place does to you?"

MacDara didn't respond. Kate's question was rhetorical. They weren't staying in Derry. They were only passing through on their way to Eglinton. But MacDara couldn't resist giving the old city a lookover. Circling the Diamond he headed back down Shipquay Street, around the Guildhall and towards Craigavon Bridge. They crossed Lough Foyle and took the road to Eglinton.

The Poetry

The Early Years

Childhood Hills

As rain falls
in the quiet evening
on these New York mountains,
my mind goes back
to other hills,

The green and purple, heathery
hills of Derry; I wonder:
do they still ruin their hard-earned
shoes kicking the loose stony
roads on the daily miles
from Craigbrack school?

Do they still hide behind the ditch and
stone the zinc roof of Ferguson's
byre, running away with hearts
thumping, while angry fists
are shaken in the summer air?

Is there a Johnny today who knocks
the bungs out of the stacked tar barrels,
and watches with glee while
other children jump the tarry river and

Childhood Hills

try to clean the mess from
shoes and clothes, knowing
that a caning awaits at home?

And is there a Charlie, deadly accurate
with a flat-stone, who can throw
one at the speeding swallow,
watch it turn and bank
into the second stone: to fall
among distant heather;
one less for Capustrano?

Pat Mullan

Craw

I was born in Craw
on a hill-farm in the heather
of an Ulster mountain

The old people said my great-grandfather
had built the first wee house there: a craw,
a thatched-roofed pighouse made of scraws.
And named these hills forever.

But you won't find Craw on any map;
the townland, the postal district
and the parish:
none of them are Craw.

On a clear day you can see Slieve Snacht,
the mountain of snow, over there
in Donegal. They say my mother's father
came from there. They called him

Wee Cocky. They said it was because
he was so dapper. But I knew different.
Craw stared across the Foyle in envy
at Donegal, the Free State.

Childhood Hills

Craw: 1944

I'm only five years old today
and I'm standing in the rain
listening   as it
dances on the roof
and falls in sheets
into a puddled river
at my feet

I know this rain will never end
and the sun will never shine again
I know the world is going to end
and I will never smile again

I'll never see
those dogfights in the air again
or look in awe down Quigley's brae
to see that Spitfire's grave
I'll never see the blackout
shut out the dead of night
and I'll never see the tilley lamp
pumped up to that bright light

I know the world is going to end
and I will never smile again.

Pat Mullan

The Lie

I don't remember now
how old I was then,
maybe five or six,
just the time when
the world is filled
with wondrous things.

Mine was a gold sovereign,
small and round, as rich
in color as country butter.
To me it was as rare
as a moon rock   it held
the promise of the future

Until one day
the Parish Priest arrived and
turned my mother all busy
and important   I was
forgotten   I didn't know
the things they talked about

I wanted to show off
my gold sovereign   so
that the priest would know

Childhood Hills

that I was important too
but I stumbled and it rolled away.

I cried and cried
I couldn't find my magic coin.
The Priest searched   on his knees
all in vain.
They tried to console me
all in vain.

In later years when
I had found and lost   other things
my mother confessed
that she had given   my magic coin
to the Priest to make
a new gold chalice.

Pat Mullan

The Quarry Hole

I imagine him now.
Swimming, floating, sinking
under water, octopus-like growth
caressing his legs, his tail;
his coat as sleek as an otters.

In winter children skate
on its icy surface
risking all on that thin floor
that separates
this life from the next.

I wasn't home the day
my father put my dog away,
tying him in a sack, weighing
him down with stones, dumping
him in the quarry   to sink
in that bottomless pit
for a crime he didn't commit.

I imagine him now
his trusting eyes staring
in that strange world   looking
for me waiting as always
for the resurrection.

Childhood Hills

I watched the sack surface
bloated, distended, pregnant,
raising my hopes
I crawled to the edge and stretched
with the forked branch   until
I reached   but the sack ruptured
spilling out its rotting cats.

I resolved that day that
I will be cremated when I die.

Pat Mullan

Against the Blue Sky

I.

Wakened,
Startled,
my head
in heather

Fuzzy
from the summer sun
and sleep
not wanted

The sound,
high-pitched,
above
in the blue

A speck,
standing still
and yet,
a flutter

Of wings
betrayed
the lark, fixed
in the cloud like

Childhood Hills

A single
polkadot.
Its song ended,
stillness again

Only
the breeze
brushing the heather,
the lark

Dropped
a mile straight down
and hung
suspended

From
the blue ceiling,
fluttered and
fell again

Like
a stone obeying
gravity, into
the bog.

II.

Naked,
trapped
like a fly
in a web.

Pat Mullan

Cornered
in that walled
backyard
in my home town.

Beneath
the black bird
suspended above,
its blades

Whirring,
almost purring,
against
the blue sky,   I

Cowered
as it dropped
straight
down

Seeking
its prey
in the streets
of my home town.

Childhood Hills

We Never Talked

I watched his adam's apple
                rise and fall
And his neck, rubbery
                on the dead snoring head.

I watched him sleep the evenings away,
Tired from the day's toil.
We never talked.
But what would we have talked about?
His football pools; he never won
My fear at school; the leather strap:
His cruel side would not have understood.

I watched him hunched nightly
                at the rosary
His rump, fetal
Droning the prayers
Like some prenatal chant.

I watched my father grow old and
I never knew him.

Pat Mullan

Sundays

They dressed up only on Sundays
to walk up the street to the cathedral,
a few pennies thrown on the table,
then they entered, blessing their
foreheads with fingertips wet from
the holy water.   Strangely erect,
they moved to their own pews,
claimed from years of Sunday use.

I remember yours:
under the pulpit to
hear the sermon better and
still
        good enough to see who
        might be wearing a new
        hat in the front row.

Mea culpa,
        Mea culpa,
                Mea maxima culpa:
You intoned louder than anyone,
like a contest that gave
rewards
        in this life and in the next.
Through my fault,
        Through my fault,
                Through my most grievous fault.

Childhood Hills

My father knelt in his
Sunday suit with a handkerchief
on the hard kneeling board to
protect the blue serge while
you purged yourself of the
World of the Flesh that you
endured and suffered.

Pat Mullan

Enslaved

I tiptoed   up
the center aisle of the
cavernous cathedral
careful   not to let my iron-tips
                touch the tiled floor
I waited   in the shadows cast
by the imperious wrought-iron lights
chained   above me
I found a pew
halfway-up   so that I
                could spy
on the confession boxes
hidden   in shadowed
                alcoves

"Hail Mary, full of grace"   loudly prayed
                                 an old lady,
                                 hair in a bun,
just like my grandmother.
The soft light silhouetted her,
hiding the worn black wool coat,
shoulders hunched   gnarled knuckles
                       firmly clasping
                       the rosary beads.
Penance to her God.

Childhood Hills

At the little shrine on the left
a young woman   lit
                        a candle
trying hard to insert it
in the wax-encrusted holder
under the mutilated Jesus,
                blood dripping from His
                slashed red heart.
Petitioning her God.

Suddenly I wanted to scream:
why   isn't our God a God of joy
why   don't we worship like our black Baptist brothers
why   are we still enslaved?

Pat Mullan

Soul Food

That old Spillar's flour bag fed me
and clothed me and educated me.

I used to look at the letter 'T' on that flour bag
and rub my finger down my cheeks

(before I could talk) to say
that that old 'T' was my dad's razor.

One day you bleached out my 'T' and all the other letters,
and dyed that old flour bag navy,

cut out a pattern and made me a smart looking suit
for my first day at school.

And you used the flour to fill our house with the smell
of baking,
the soda bread, the treacle bread, the oat farls and the fadge.

Our soul food.

Childhood Hills

Bicycle Ride

I sat on the cold handlebars
my thighs bone-tight to the metal
as you pushed me

Your breath spluttered
hot on my neck
like the engine in
your old Morris Minor

Up and up that brae
you pushed till you seemed
to stand still on the pedals
almost waiting to fall

Hailstones beat down
on my bare legs
till they were scourged red
but I don't remember the pain

I only remember your strength
and your closeness.
We were never like that again.

Pat Mullan

The Champions

We stayed up till two in the morning,
waiting for the opening round.

Madison Square Garden, I believe.
Such a grand sounding name to me.

Joe Louis vs. Ezzard Charles, what
kind of a name is Ezzard, I thought.

The wireless was a Marconi, I believe,
with carbide batteries, no electricity

And I could see the suspense in the eyes
of my father and my grandfather too.

Suspense and silence and the roar
of the crowd three thousand miles away.

Joe Louis, the Brown Bomber, what
is a Brown Bomber, I thought.

Childhood Hills

But I could see the reverence in their eyes
when I mentioned his name, like a god,

Someone who could conquer the world for us,
Someone who could make us feel like champions.

Pat Mullan

Uncle Peter

That last photo of Uncle Peter
taken in Cairo
       when he was an Irish Guard
Six-three and ramrod straight
       you could imagine the busby

Three years in a stalag
I remember
       the plate in the skull
of his fellow Guardsman
       shot when he was captured

And his escapes
Stealing
       the pig's food from the farmers
Milking
       the goats and rolling it into a ball

And his recapture
Staked out
       in a shallow pit in the sun

Childhood Hills

Blindfolded
      to be shot and then to live

I remember my awe
turning to fear
      when his eyes stared
Wildly
      into the leaping fireplace flames
They told me he was shellshocked

In my teens I only knew he was
In Gransha
      that place you didn't talk about
The Asylum
      where they were kept away from the world

They said he went to war again
Set fire
      to his mother's roof
Tried
      to burn out the enemy

Pat Mullan

They said I was his favourite
Used to take me
        on his knees to feed me
So handsome
        in his uniform

They said he tried to flee
at Plymouth (or was it Portsmouth?)
but they didn't know that
he only wanted to be a policeman.

The Bird

Moo-lan, where's Doo-lan today?
He's ill, Father. But you proved
that I didn't know and you gave
me six with your leather strap:

Quod erat demonstrandum.

You played tic-tac-toe
on free class periods: you always won.
Your soutane became a devil's triangle
for pens, pennies, and pencils:

Our coerced bets.

You banged our heads with
Hall's big red textbook—
to teach us algebra; instead

you taught us dread.

Pat Mullan

In the evenings I watched you
pace our study hall like a hawk,
with your broken nose and turned-in toes,
while your breviary hid a Mickey Spillane novel.

We called you The Bird.

Small Victory

Some nights we went over the wall
into the Bogside   and then
just sat   smoked our butts
and felt a small victory at

Cheating the system of rules
and laws   other nights
we walked alone or in
twos and threes   inside

Feeling less   free
but out of the reach of
the grim study halls
and the priests who

Strapped education into
our hands
and intimidation into
our heads

Till we were molded for ever
or fought back and left
to apprentice in stores:
no room for Greek or Latin there.

Pat Mullan

Paddington Station

Did I ever tell you about the
                night I spent
in the men's room
                at Paddington station?

Thrown there out of Euston,
your gaping immigrant mouth.
Clattered through the bowels
of your black smoke-stacked north.
Beyond Paddington to Hammersmith.
Joe Loss and his orchestra.
The haven of your paddies.
Even then, late fifties time,
One cold room,
        No Irish or Coloured
        Three by foured
        on your vacancies;
Ever vacant for me.
No Great Gael, just
your paddy.

Did I ever tell you about the
                night I spent
in the men's room
                at Paddington station?

The Later Years

Paris

A pernod on the Champs Elysee,
Life observed in Montparnasse,
A brief flirtation in La Coupole
Fills my mind as I
Watch her stroll
Into view on the boulevard;
Her body moves in complement:
Lyrics composed to music
              to Paris

She pauses at the newsstand,
Profiled with Le Monde,
Nipples free and pressed
        against the fabric
             of Paris

She turns as breezes mold
Her thigh, and
Moves towards me. I
Hope. The guitar strummed by the
        American boy attracts her ear.
Her face shows joy
             to Paris

Childhood Hills

And to me. Two tables away
She joins her friend, the girl
With the high green boots.
They kiss and blend, a
        Toulouse-Lautrec, a
                living canvas.

My palette ready: a little
Rouge on her high cheek
Bones. The flower seller
Points to me as her fingers
                hold one red rose.

She smiles, takes my
Offering and lays it
                on the table.

Pat Mullan

The Dancer

Your tall limbs moved
Rhythmically to the beat,
Forming nubile columns
Under innocent buttocks

Transfixing
The shadowed faces like
A pendulum held
By an unseen hypnotist.

Your face, framed in flaxen,
Windswept,
Betrayed no sign
Of premed study in neurobiology.

Childhood Hills

The Turning Point

I see you at the window
on Central Park South.   The first snow
is   falling   and you talk of   leaving,
            your time has come

But how can that be, we've only met
You are Spring to me and I want
to feel the hot Summer sun

You speak of sorrows   and
give me your   love
I sit enraptured as your poems
find my   soul   and
         change me   forever

You are with me now
turning my solitude
into a symphony; your heart
            is my conductor

I am writing again

Pat Mullan

April Sixteenth

If he were here, he'd be here,
those Runyon matches said,
but I've no doubt that Damon's world
is still inside my head

I wander through the memories
of that April day we met
Over sizzlers and Mondavi,
were we trying to forget?

Or was Runyon's just the high ground
that most will never gain
and you and I got lucky
while fleeing from the pain?

Hampton Sunset

The evening sky painted itself
in hues of red and orange,
while unseen waves
caressed the catamarans
with gentle slaps.

A lone gull, astray,
glided overhead
like
the Ancient Mariner's albatross

But it cast no shadow
when you stood, a sentinel
silently manning the ramparts
of your own Highland place.

The charcoal embers,
gusted by the breeze,
sparked like shooting stars.
You had found peace
in these dying days of summer.

Pat Mullan

The Gamble

The key to our room at Caesar's Palace
hangs over our wine-bar now
like a trophy hunted down
in some exotic place.

It hangs there to remind me
of nights in the Nevada desert
when we gambled

Our future together   tossing
a coin and not waiting to see
if it came up heads or tails.

Childhood Hills

For Seamus Heaney

You held them fast
in the Donnell library
that February in New York.
The Derry softness, unchanged.

Twenty-five years ago
we boarded at St. Columb's,
our lonely scarp, where we had rights
on the English lyric and, all around us,
you named it, the Ministry of Fear.

Your words command
in this sophisticated place.
Your elegy to Robert Lowell
as strongly reverent as your Casualty.

Question me this, Seamus Heaney:
was it the strap in the big study hall
or our fear of Tierney that dragged
us silent from the Derry bogs and
paraded us on the world's stage.

Pat Mullan

The Town I Love so Well...

(with apologies to Phil Coulter)

Derry: 1966 Scene I

"Okay, out of the car, Chief!"
My God, this is real, I thought. I let the passport go, and eased myself onto the road. The scruffy one examined my New York driver's license. The lanky one, with the rifle, peered over his shoulder
"What's this 'ere, mate?"
"It's my driver's license"
"You American, then?"
But he didn't wait for an answer.
"Open the boot there, Chief!"

I fumbled in my pocket, found my keys and moved to the rear of the car. The first key was the wrong one, the second turned the lock.

"Open it all the way, Chief!"
"Now, move back!"
The lanky one stood aside, rifle pointed belligerently.
"What's this then, Chief?"
Lanky pointed to the long cardboard box with the shamrock on its side.
"Some liquor I bought at Shannon"
"Take it out and open it, Chief!"
I obeyed and they let me close the boot. When I left they were advancing on the car behind me.

Childhood Hills

Derry: 1974 Scene II

She tripped ahead
enthusiastic; unaware
of the broken walls and
battle-thrown rubble strewn there.

She was blond, two years old and
my daughter. Born free,
a child of America in her father's
town. Her heart could not see

The emptiness; black ugly gaps
where homes once stood
and the fear that lurked behind
windows now covered with wood.

A man staggered out
from some mean doorway
and, fortified against reality,
eyed my daughter, to say:

"Get the wee girl in
or them pigs'll shoot her"
She smiled in that no-man's land
between the man and a pair

Of running, tatooed paras,
the vanguard of a duck squad,
eight strong, yet showing fear,
in pursuit of a fleeing Bogside lad

Pat Mullan

Who, joined by a companion,
taunted them, threw a rock
and fled again. I grabbed my daughter,
now afraid, and ran a block

From memory, to William Street
to stand in shock and disbelief;
no houses stood where I remembered,
only broken gables in relief.

My daughter ran ahead again;
she'll never know my lovely town
or suffer at the hands of those
who cut the Oak Grove down.

Derry: 1974 Scene III

It stopped, hurt by the red brick wall,
crimson now and less symmetrical.

Its victim lay, face broken
in the surreal silence of the crowd,

Halted like a jungle when danger threatens.
The armoured car moves in like a great blind bull.

Soldiers spring out like panthers and
children scurry like rats from darkened doorways.

Childhood Hills

The gutter turns red, coloring this gray Victorian place:
a midden of rusting cars, broken bottles and

one plastic bullet.

Derry: 1978 Scene IV

The fixed check-points were gone
this time   and they waved me on

at the border customs in Muff;
they seemed tired   like they'd had enough

people lingered down the Strand
or chatted   hand in hand

and children played on the street again
laughing gaily as they ran

past the single British soldier
in the doorway   his morning stand

Davey's pub was filled that night
with the locals out for their evening pint

as my brother talked of Paddy Galvin
and his poetry reading   in the Gweedore bar

my cousin just back from the Sligo Flad Ceol
told of travels   near and far

Pat Mullan

the merits of Tom Paxton   and the war
while Gudrun spoke of her German beer

and people showed less fear
than seventy-four   when I was last here.

Derry: 1995 Scene V

Yes, yes! I see the new shopping malls
and the Mercs and BMWs on the Strand,
and the Rich down the Culmore Road
live just like the Rich of any land.

Yes, yes! I see the new Foyle Bridge,
see its spine   curve towards the sky
but is it the bridge to the future
or is it just another lie?

Question me this, Seamus Heaney:
was it the strap in St. Columb's big study hall
or our fear of the priests that dragged
us silent from these Derry bogs and
threatened to make atheists of us all.

Coulter said he loved this town
and he said there was music here;
you said we had rights on the English lyric,
and all around us, you named it,
the Ministry of Fear.

Childhood Hills

The concrete barriers are gone now,
and the traffic nips and tacks
through each roundabout,
flowing freely out and away
                        I don't look back.

Pat Mullan

Uijongbu

He stared at us:
Intruders.
His face, weather-worn:
Inscrutable.

We trudged, single-file:
Uncaring.
We looked, right through:
Incurious.

His feet in muddy water:
Correct.
Toil-worn pants rolled to knees:
Timeless.

Our olive-greens, dusty:
Foreign.
Rifles shoulder-slung, empty:
Protectors.

His eyes, small, (seemed) sad:
Resentment.
Bare arms, sinewy, blend:
Belong.

We pass, uninvited:
Untouched.
He stoops, unbending:
Ageless.

Childhood Hills

The Elevator

Forgive yourself

Scratched into the door
with some pointed instrument
it etched itself
into the closed space
as we moved

Downward
from floor to floor
I watched   from my corner
each new passenger   face ahead
into the closing doors as they revealed

The message

I watched as   the eternity
between points of embarkation
transformed
a sagging chin to one more firm
a melancholy eye to one less dim
The youthful slouching shoulder
on at ten
somehow seemed so straight
at seven

Pat Mullan

The Bank

I should feel that I have it made now sitting in this boardroom
seven floors above the bank, gold in the vault below.

And yet my pen is not a spade and this bank does not produce
wet peat to fire my memories.

Twenty years ago my own turf bank
lay out in the bogland, a mile from the house

Where I wielded the right-angled spade
with the full energy of my twelve years

And lofted wet peat onto the heathery bank,
in rows left open for the summer sun and wind to dry.

Three spadefulls deep into the hard clay ground,
I'd stand with aching back and sweaty brow, to imagine

The faces of the old storytellers, in from the cold,
glowing from the fire in those bricks of black gold.

Exoggle

My brother was in France
when John died and he cried
because he wasn't there at John's side.

John was my brother's neighbor,
for years farming his lonely acreage,
creating life from that hilly land in Donegal.

He lived alone, he never wed,
the animals were his closest friends and
he farmed the images in his head.

He'd been up late the night I met him,
a cow had given birth and he'd helped
the newborn calf stand up on its spindly legs.

I see him now by the open fire,
chest bared on the coldest of days,
eyes closed and mind conjuring up

New words, a new language
fertilized and harvested in his mind,
just like a good year's planting.

"Do you get the point?"
he'd say to me, never opening his eyes,
but looking through me just the same.

Pat Mullan

"Exoggle! You can't exoggle your way out of that"
and he'd given me a new word, a new thought,
a new way to say something

"You can close the book on that"
he'd say, with conviction, and you knew
there was nothing more to be said

We're experimenting today,
modifying the genes in the food we grow.
John would be horrified at that

I can hear him say:
"We'll exoggle ourselves into a corner,
just like a rat."

Childhood Hills

Looking for Hemingway

Maybe I even sat where you sat,
at that bar in Sloppy Joe's.
What were you drinking?
I imagine it had to be the 'hard stuff',
undiluted, straight up.

I imagine this, just as
I imagine you, fortified with drink,
pulling that urinal out of the wall
and carrying it, just like Jesus,
home on your shoulder
in the middle of the night.

Do you know that the tourists
look at it now, derisively.
Planted by your wife, prettied
by its tile border, it waters
your seven-toed cats. I'll bet
you'd have left it in Sloppy's
if you'd known it would all end like this.

You wrote some of your best
work in this house on Key West,
that's what they say.

Pat Mullan

But where did you find the time
to cross that bridge
to your writing place?
Weren't you out there,
fishing by day, and in here,
drinking by night?

I want to understand you
as I stand here
in your bedroom
between
your ceramic Picasso
and your Spanish birthing stool.

You should have died here
in Key West, or
in your home in Cuba, or
out at sea, or
in Italy during the war, or
gored by a noble bull, or
mauled by an African lion

But, no,
you had to end it all
in Ketchum, Idaho,
a soul-less sounding place.
Did Beckett write your epitaph?

Childhood Hills

Edinburgh

Those who know say
you're the Athens of the North

But the Parthenon is ravaged by time
yet your castle stands muscular in its prime

One room where James was born, is
preserved, like an empty womb, waiting;

While another room, a shrine to Culloden,
reminds us that it's not forgotten.

The Celtic Crosses on your battlements,
mute as tombstones, toll your foreign dead.

The Stone of Scone is back on Scottish soil
and Braveheart's spirit haunts it all.

On Princes Street scaffold-splints mend your wounds
and the evening light seems to lift your gloom.

And you wait there proud, your time has come,
the past is past, its course has run.

Pat Mullan

The Elegant Crane
for Kazuhiro Moriyama

I've been to your Japan.
Once, long ago, I
landed at Tachikawa
and drove madly through
the night to Yokohama.

But that's only a memory.
So long ago, sometimes
it seems that I've
imagined it, until now

Watching your fingers
deftly fold and fold again
the square of gaily colored paper
into this surprise

This elegant crane
that sits here now
on my desk in Connemara,
connecting East to West.

Conversations with Caitlin
my seven year old daughter

Cait, you do a lot of thinking,
don't you?

Yes, Dad. That's what I was just thinking about.
I was thinking that I have a lot of
filing cabinets in my head.

Dad, how deep are the caves?
How far are the stars?

Pat Mullan

Leaving

"You've done your share of leaving, son"
my mother said   reproaching and yet respecting
wanting me to stay   but willing me to go.

Childhood Hills

Granny Bunty's Button Box

Buttons of all colors,
shapes and sizes

Danced in Granny Bunty's
button box

Sliding through her
searching fingers

Each hoping to be
the chosen one

Caitlin stands at
Granny's knee

She's almost two and
she can see

The buttons come alive,
like magic

Granny's looking for a
button that's blue

She finds one and
then finds two

Pat Mullan

Caomhe* counts them
once again

Granny Bunty now
has ten

Enough for both their dresses
then

* phonetically: *Keefa*

Childhood Hills

Savages

When I first saw you, you were a painted savage
riding down on the circled wagons,

your arrows showering death,
scalps like medals on your belt.

We cheered in that cinema when the bugle sounded,
and the cavalry rode to the rescue

and you ran away leaving
your dead face down on the ground.

I met you again in the Zane Grey westerns of my teens
and later watched you die in The Last of the Mohicans

and, even later, when my romance with America began
Geronimo and Cochise were legends in your land

In my seven years in Florida your Miccosukees taught me well
and showed me how the Seminoles survived their hell

Pat Mullan

forging a separate life, salting their hearts and
soldering their souls forever to tree and stump and
hammock.

No Hollywood lies can ever destroy the dignity of
Sitting Bull
or paint a savage mind from the words of Chief Seattle

*the ashes of my ancestors are sacred
and their resting place is hallowed ground*

I weep today when I think of you, Choctaws,
forced out of your rich Mississippi land

thousands dying on your *Trail of Tears* to Oklahoma,
burned by the roadside, ground too frozen to bury you

yet, only sixteen years later, when we were dying,
from famine, in our thousands by the roadside

you sent us $710 and whatever corn and food you
could spare,
which makes me wonder about all that we share

Childhood Hills

maybe your *Kowi anukasha,* your playful little people, belong to
the same world as our own little people, our *leprechauns*

and maybe your spirit *Ishkitini* that warns of death
can hear the wailing of our own *banshee.*

Pat Mullan

You always Wondered

You know there was no-one in the bedroom
when you felt your way in the darkness to the toilet.
They say there's a cold feeling in the air
when there's another presence in the room
but you convinced yourself that it was natural
to feel a cold chill in January.

She didn't stir on her side of the bed.
You always woke up quietly.
You always slid your feet out onto the cold floor
and eased the rest of your body out
without tugging the bedclothes.
She never knew that you went to the toilet
three times during the night.
You never told her.
You didn't want her to know
that your body was beginning to show
the signs of wear.

You never flushed the toilet at night.
The filling tank made too much noise.
It would surely wake her up.
She always left her watch on the glass shelf by the sink.
That's the only way you knew the time.
But you really didn't want to know the time.

Childhood Hills

You always left your own watch
on the side table by your bed, in the dark
where you couldn't read it till daybreak.

You groped behind you with your right hand
and found the hot water bottle
that she had put in your side of the bed.
It was tepid now at three in the morning.
You slid under the duvet and pulled it up
so that your head was covered, just enough
to hide you but not enough to suffocate you.
You turned over on your left side so that
your good left ear was silenced by the pillow.
Your deaf right ear didn't matter.

You lay there as you did every night,
trying to get back to sleep.
Eventually you did return to sleep
but never to the dream you were in before you woke up.
She was always awake before you.
You would wake up to the feeling
of her arm around your waist,
her loins warm against the small of your back
and her lips brushing the nape of your neck.
You always turned over and blessed your good fortune
as your arms encircled her body and
you kissed her gently on her eyelids,
the tip of her nose, and her soft inviting lips.

Pat Mullan

You always wondered
what she would do that morning when you didn't respond.
That morning you were certain would come
when she would wake up,
stretch and turn around to encircle your waist
and brush her lips against your cold, cold neck.
That morning when you wouldn't turn over to hold her.
That last morning of your life.
You always wondered about that.

You were still wondering
when you realized you were awake.
It was morning and the light was filtering into the bedroom.
You had wakened by yourself this morning.
You turned and looked over.
She was still asleep.
You felt as though you had been given a gift today.
The gift of morning that she always brought to you.
You would bring it to her.
You turned over and circled her waist with your arm.
You brushed your lips against her cold, cold neck.

Childhood Hills

On the Way to Connemara
(with apologies to W.B. Yeats)

A funny thing happened on the way to Connemara when I met the young lady on the Costa Golf Course in the designer jogging suit with her ears wrapped in a Sony Walkman her right hand pumping the phallic steel of the latest fad while her left hand fed her Jane Fonda body thousands of units of stress vitamins from a naturally clear intravenous like straw that parted her Aspen toned lips and connected with a non-biodegradable container emblazoned in the pastel blues and pinks of Florida....

    I will arise and go now and go to Connemara where time goes dropping slow and live where the air is filled with linnets wings and poteen stills abound in the bee loud glades

    I will arise and go now

    It's time for me to go now

    It's
              time
                      for
                              me
                                    to
                                          go
                                              now....

Introducing
Annemarie Mullan Whilton

Childhood Hills

...her voice at age fifteen

Pat Mullan

My Cat

Lazy wisp of cotton
cuddly, cozy,
soft and shy
generating warmth.
Metamorphosis:
like a spy,
cunningly quick,
on soft cushioned pads;
Pert ears,
glowing coal eyes,
spitfire tongue
when mad.

Eyes

Pools of living color
Fathomless depths of the soul
Book without a cover
Speech without words
Answers without a question
Verdict without a jury
Wound without a bandage

Revealing all

Pat Mullan

Grass

Fresh from the mother earth
Crisp and cold
The defiant crunch
of shattered echoes
on a still misty morning
Its dew-dipped blades
reach out to the sky
stretch and yearn
A single wet round tear
inexorably slips down
the green parallel strip
The sun peeks out
Acute edges smoothen
A soothing swish
is heard
The whisper of contentment
is born
as the wind
slowly caresses by.

Storm

Cold hatred
Zeus, dreaded thunderbolts
rumble of the clouds
violent piercing slash
Split seams of the heavens
Harsh cutting rain
and the silent bitterness
that follows.

Pat Mullan

Obituary

On March 8, 1981,
Annemarie Mullan
died,
She left a final farewell to
her family
and friends,
her cousin,
knick-knacks,
pizza with sausages,
100,000 orthodontic rubberbands,
old raggedy Ann,
collection of seashells,
numerous perfumes,
charcoal sketches,
the smell of gasoline,
painted canvasses, and
strawberry cheesecake icecream,
and to all: the things that
made up the threads
of the severed rope
of her life.

Childhood Hills

...and her voice in more recent days

Pat Mullan

Monday Morning

You open your eyes
To the stillness of the room

Walk the dog
Her urine hissing green streams.

You drive your car
To the sounds of Coltraine.

Looking left
The city will alight.

Bearing right,
The traffic will part.

You are awake
Quickly, quickly, quickly now

The day
It awaits you.

Your First Day at Dollys

I left you there on Thursday
And your sister cried.
I watched you run
from swing to swing,
not getting a turn.
You found your space
in the confines
of a fluorescent orange car,
and you maniacally wheeled it
alone in delight.
As your sister cried.

I felt full of your sister's fears
and your joy.
Like a buoy
afloat on swelling seas,
Attached to my
now-sightless cargo.
Like an umbilical cord
stretched,
Adrift and lonely
and a little proud.

I pulled out of the parking lot
as your sister cried,
Don't leave her.

Pat Mullan

My Dad is Home

Twelve Bens.
Mini dragons.
Clock innards sprung
over heathered hills.
Silent to the Queen's
clicked patent heels.

Twelve Bens.
Sleeping beasts,
Hoarder of Celtic bones
under purpled hue.
Sacred to the farmer's
turf shodden shoe.

Twelve Bens.
Burdened camel.
Backbone to German
racing bikes.
Pass over the horseman's
bloodied tracks.

In Memoriam: James Dickey

About James Dickey

In addition to his novel *Deliverance* James Dickey wrote approximately 20 volumes of poetry. Among his works of poetry were *Drowning With Others* (1962), *Buckdancer's Choice* (1966), which won the National Book Award, *The Eye-Beaters* (1970), *The Zodiac* (1976), *Scion* (1980), *Puella* (1982), and *The Central Motion* (1983). In 1972 he wrote the screenplay for the film adaptation of *Deliverance* and in 1977 he composed a poem, *The Strength of Fields,* for Jimmy Carter's Presidential Inauguration.

Born in a suburb of Atlanta on February 2, 1923, the son of Eugene and Maibelle Swift Dickey, James Dickey grew up with a love of football, canoeing, archery and other high-action, high-risk activities. In 1942, he enlisted in the Army Air Corps and served in World War II. During this time he began to write but it wasn't until the Korean War that he sold his first poem *Shark in the Window* to *The Swanee Review*.

James Dickey eventually became poetry consultant to the Library of Congress. In 1968 he became poet in residence and professor of English at the University of South Carolina. He died on January 19, 1997.

James Dickey's Poetry: The Religious Dimension

But let me say that I have always been against traditional religion because my religion has been so personal to me. I always felt that God and I have a very good understanding, and the more the ritualistic services go on, the more God and I stand by and laugh. I don't believe that the God that created the universe has any interest in the dreadful kind of self-abasement men go through in religious ceremonies. (1).

Those are the words of James Dickey. They sound strong and unequivocal: he totally rejects traditional religion and the established forms of ritual worship associated with it. He is egotistical and presumptuous enough to vilify those who participate in religious ceremonies and to place himself on an equal level with God. Such ego! Such confidence! One would immediately assume that here was a man who had made up his mind and who possessed none of the doubts that most humans do. No search for God seems necessary for Dickey—he has found Him and they have a "very good understanding". (2). James Dickey has been searching for God all his life and it permeates his poetry; he finds Him too, finds Him everywhere and accords God a stature and a mystique that truly identifies with traditional religious beliefs. "He can start anywhere and find god," writes Norman Silverstein, "not god, with a small g, but the Lord who creates, intercedes, and aids." (3).

---

(1). James Dickey, *Self-Interviews*, (New York, 1970), p. 78.
(2). Ibid.
(3). Norman Silverstein, *"James Dickey's Muscular Eschatology"*, *Contemporary Poetry in America*, (New York, 1974), p. 306

Childhood Hills

Many of Dickey's poems deal with his total preoccupation with all things, especially nature (of which he writes much); through nature he reflects God's work of creation. According to Arthur Gregor, "Dickey deals with the magic that results when the observer sees the supernatural expressed in nature, and experiences—is ultimately involved in—this transformation." (4)

Dickey's view of God and creation is not a simple, untroubled one, but rather, a vision of loftiness, supernatural themes and of man's unity with the universe. In his poem *"Inside the River"* (5) he starts off with someone gently edging one foot and then the other into a river, seemingly to bathe or wade. Before the poem ends though, the person has entered the river, evoking a sense of total immersion, almost the biblical form of baptism. The river is a symbol of immortality as these lines show:

> Put on the river
> Like a fleeing coat,
> A garment of motion,
> Tremendous, immortal.

and the dead are also immortal as in :

> Live like the dead
> In their flying feeling.

and again, towards the end of the poem, when birth and death are united by the grasp of a root:

---

(4) Arthur Gregor, "*James Dickey, American Romantic,*" ***James Dickey: The Expansive Imagination*** (Florida, 1973), p. 77

(5) James Dickey, ***Poems 1957-1967*** (New York, 1974), p. 105

> Weight more changed
> Than that of one
> Now being born,
> Let go the root.
> Move with the world
> As the deep dead move,
> Opposed to nothing.

Dickey's identity with traditional religious reference points marks the strong presence of God and creation expressed through his poem, "*In the Mountain Tent*" (6), which describes the poet's innermost mingling with nature whilst lying inside a tent during a heavy rainstorm. Here he describes the shining of water "like dark, like light, out of Heaven" and uses images such as "the sustained intake of all breath before the first word of the Bible" and "the tent taking shape on my body like ill-fitting, Heavenly clothes." The ending lines of the poem have a christ-like image of resurrection as he says:

> From holes in the ground comes my voice
> In the God-silenced tongue of the beasts.
> "I shall rise from the dead," I am saying.

Dickey describes this poem as one in which the man in the tent, while lying there, begins the dream of his own death. Being a product of western culture, the man is influenced by Christian doctrines and the belief in the Resurrection. And he, therefore, feels kinship with the animals on the mountainside and a fundamental difference in that he realizes he may rise from the dead and they'll only die. (7)

---

(6) James Dickey, *Poems 1957-1967* (New York, 1974), p. 109
(7) James Dickey, *Self-Interviews* (New York, 1970), p. 120

Childhood Hills

In the words of Peter Davison, "Dickey's work is a search, in a sense, for heaven on earth," (8) Dickey never crosses the supernatural boundary to lend imagery in his poetry to that heaven in the afterlife. When he does deal with such a heaven, he reserves it for the animals in *"The Heaven of Animals".* (9) It is not the conceptual human heaven of harps and white robes but is expressed as a continuance of the animals' lives in their natural environment. Dickey can best perceive or imagine what would be an ideal animal heaven—simply the continuity of their earthly existence :

> Here they are. The soft eyes open.
> If they have lived in a wood
> It is a wood.
> If they have lived on plains
> It is grass rolling
> Under their feet forever.

Dickey does not seem to be able to perceive or imagine what would be an ideal human heaven, so he does not deal with it. This is another example of his unresolved conflict with the traditional religious concepts of his childhood. "The Dantean comic end, a heaven for people, does not enter into Dickey's poetry. It might be that it carries for him (out of a Southern Bible Belt culture) connotations of spiritual fixedness," (10) writes Robert W. Hill.

---

(8) Peter Davison, *"The Great Grassy World from Both Sides,"* **James Dickey: The Expansive Imagination** (Florida, 1973), p. 46

(9) James Dickey, *Poems 1957-1967* (New York, 1974), p. 59

(10) Robert W. Hill, *"James Dickey: Comic Poet,"* **James Dickey: The Expansive Imagination** (Florida, 1973), p. 148

Despite the innumerable Biblical references in his poetry, Dickey disclaims any religious identification: "I love the Bible, though. But the Bible to me is a great work of literature only." (11) He is, however, imbued with religion (his own brand as he defines it):

> But the religious sense, which seems to me
> very strong in my work in some weird kind of
> way, is a very personal kind of stick-and-stone
> religion. I would have made a great Bushman
> or an aborigine who believes that spirits inhabit
> all things. (12)

This personal religion of Dickey's is Christian, paganistic, Hindu-like, and primitive: a cauldron of supernatural potions that creates in the poet his need to blend man and beast, natural and supernatural, reality and fantasy, into a recipe that leaves him with a fear of death (not physical death, but mortality), a search for a reincarnate continuity of existence and a need to define the state of afterlife. He separates the world created by man from that which exists naturally, yet he will not fully commit himself to either confirming or denying that it is God's world:

> I'm much more interested in a man's
> relationship to the God-made world,
> or the universe-made world than to
> the man-made world. The natural
> world seems infinitely more important
> to me than the man-made world. (13)

---

(11) James Dickey, *Self-Interviews* (New York, 1970), p. 78
(12) Ibid., p. 79
(13) Ibid., p. 67

Childhood Hills

The theme of resurrection from the dead and of continuity of existence through reincarnation is a magnetic attraction for Dickey. He deals with a very traditional Christian concept of resurrection in his poem, *"Sleeping Out at Easter"* (14) from the collection **Into the Stone**. According to Dickey, the poem describes a father waking up after having slept outside all night at Eastertime. When Dickey was in the advertising business, he slept out, in the springtime, in a sleeping bag in a little pine grove behind his suburban house in Atlanta. In relating that experience, which provided the idea for the poem, Dickey says:

> But I didn't wake up feeling that I was Christ. That's something I made up. Still, reading the poem again, I feel that I should have awakened on Easter thinking I was Christ, in the same sense that every man is Christ and Christ is every man, if you're a believer. (15)

Just as James Dickey cannot (and does not wish to) separate himself from his Southern background and identity, neither can he separate himself from his traditional Southern religious roots and early beliefs, as he pronounces that he has:

> Church always seemed to me to be very much beside the point. Religion to me involves myself and the universe, and it does not admit of any kind of intermediary, such as Jesus or the Bible. (16)

---

(14) James Dickey, *Poems 1957-1967* (New York, 1974), p. 17
(15) James Dickey, *Self-Interviews* (New York, 1970), p. 85
(16) Ibid., p. 78

Pat Mullan

The pronounced rejection of Jesus is strongly contested by the poetic incorporation of Christ in poems like "*Sleeping Out at Easter*" and "*Walking on Water*", (17) another poem from the collection, **Into the Stone**. This poem is literally a narrative about a boy crossing a river by poling while standing on a plank. However, the plank is barely submerged beneath the water and the poem becomes a refection of the supernatural Biblical ability of Christ to walk on water:

> Later, it came to be said
> That I was seen walking on water,
> Not moving my legs
> Except for the wrong step of sliding:
> A child who leaned on a staff,
> A curious pilgrim hiking
> Between two open blue worlds

Even Dickey acknowledges the theme when he describes the creative process behind "*Walking on Water*": "I thought, 'Well, let's take this seriously as a miracle.' It's a kind of natural miracle. He would seem to be like a Junior Christ." (18) This theme (of Christ walking on water) is also contained in the poem "*The Lifeguard*" (19) from the collection **Drowning with Others**. George Lensing writes, "The lifeguard, in the actions of his own consciousness, suggests the image of Christ, who also walked on waters, and was able to resurrect the dead." (20) This poem primarily concerns man's inability to undo things already done, especially to return to life those who have died, a concern that fills Dickey's

---

(17) James Dickey, *Poems 1957-1967* (New York,1974), p. 39
(18) James Dickey, *Self-Interviews* (New York, 1970), p. 97
(19) James Dickey, *Poems 1957-1967* (New York, 1974), p. 51
(20) George Lensing, "*James Dickey and the Movements of Imagination*", *James Dickey: The Expansive Imagination* (Florida, 1973), p. 168

consciousness and makes him continually aware of how seemingly unfair life can be: relationships with others, the essence of life, are but a fleeting thing owing to the mortality of all things. In *"The Lifeguard"*, Dickey describes the failure of a lifeguard to rescue a child and the guilt that overcomes him because he had also fractured the unquestioning faith of the village children who believed that he could prevent them from harm. So he hides among the boats, waiting till nighttime and hallucinating that he could walk out on the moonlight on the river and rescue the child who'd been lost:

> I set my broad sole upon silver,
> On the skin of the sky, on the moonlight,
> Stepping outward from earth onto water
> In quest of the miracle
>
> This village of children believed
> That I could perform as I dived
> For one who had sunk from my sight.

Much of Dickey's poetry emanates from personal experience and remembrance. He once participated in diving to try to recover the body of someone who had drowned. The stony feeling in his fingers is recaptured in these lines: (21)

> And my fingertips turned into stone
> From clutching immovable blackness.

Dickey, himself, commented on *"The Lifeguard"* thus: "In the delirium of grief——he comes to believe——that he'll be able to walk out into the water, much as Christ did, and raise the child back to life." (22)

---

(21) James Dickey, *Self-Interviews* (New York, 1970), p. 102
(22) Ibid., p. 103

Identifying poetic characters with Christ was always a Dickey tendency. Even in his earliest writings, he once published a long poem in **Poetry** magazine called *"The First Morning of Cancer".* In Dickey's words, it was a supposedly visionary poem about a man suffering from a brain tumor and how the affliction affected his mental processes and caused him to think and see different things. Dickey eventually had the man identify himself with Christ. (23)

Richard Howard, in writing about James Dickey, has stated that:

> The poet confronts and laments (exults over)
> the outrage of individual death, of a linear
> movement within time—each event and each
> moment being unique, therefore lost. (24)

Dickey's strong association with animal life and nature has provided the poet with a methodology for taking the poetic license of denying the reality of man's mortality and defeating "the outrage of individual death". (25) Again, Dickey must search for a religious concept to work with, reincarnation, and he said:

> Reincarnation is one religious idea I have
> always loved believing in. I don't know
> whether the soul passes from one kind of
> creature to another; I hope it does. (26)

Dickey deals with this subject in the poem, *"Reincarnation (I)"* from the **Buckdancer's Choice** collection and, again, in *"Reincarnation (II)"* from the collection in **Falling**. In neither of these poems is the man

---

(23) Ibid., p. 47
(24) Richard Howard, *Alone with America* (New York, 1969), p. 91
(25) Ibid., p. 91
(26) James Dickey, *Self-Interviews* (New York, 1970), p. 140

reincarnated again as a human and that shouldn't surprise, given the predominance of animal life as subject matter for much of Dickey's poetry. George Lensing, in reflecting on this aspect, has written:

> In all these poems Dickey suggests that the spiritual affinity between man and animals is sacred and that animal life, in its natural beauty and instinctive wisdom, is one to which humans may aspire and in which they may find their own heightened identity. (27)

"*Reincarnation (I)*" (28) is a somber, thought-provoking poem about a man being reincarnated as a rattlesnake. The narrative focuses on the natural order of life from the vantage point of the snake and, subtly, looks backward to one man's way of life. The snake exists as the poem begins and the only overt reference to a previous life appears in the first stanza:

> Still, passed through the spokes of an old wheel,
>   on and around
> The hub's furry rust in the weeds and shadows
>   of the riverbank,
> This one is feeling his life as a man move
>   slowly away.
> Fallen from that estate, he has gone down on
>   his knees
> And beyond, disappearing into the egg buried
>   under the sand

---

(27) George Lensing, "*James Dickey and the Movements of Imagination*", *James Dickey: The Expansive Imagination*, (Florida, 1973), p. 164

(28) James Dickey, *Poems 1957-1967*, (New York, 1974), p. 196

The mission of the snake becomes clear as the narrative proceeds: to lie and wait in the shadow of the old wagon wheel, poised with poisonous intent, to strike the first man to appear:

> But mainly, now, from waiting—all the time a
> symbol of evil—
> Not for food, but for the first man to walk by
> the gentle river:
> Minute by minute the head becomes more
> poisonous and poised.

In his own words, Dickey sees the rattlesnake as a symbol of justice and, in what can only be a definite Biblical reference to the Garden of Eden, states: "The justice of the Lord, in its most striking case, depended on the intervention of the snake." (29) It appears that Dickey has interwoven into this poem a cyclical process of life and death, with the snake not only being the instrument of life's continuity through reincarnation but also being the instrument of death through its poisonous fangs. In some way, Dickey also wants this poem to incorporate the justice of the Lord and the mystery of God's world as seen through the drama in the Garden of Eden, which was a place of creation, death and rebirth in a new environment.

"*Reincarnation (II)*" (30) is about an office worker who is reincarnated as a migratory sea bird. In this poem, the man realizes that he has now become a bird which is a departure from "*Reincarnation (I)*", where the snake didn't know that he had once been a man. In speaking about this poem, James Dickey has said:

---

(29) James Dickey, *Self-Interviews*, (New York, 1970), p. 141
(30) James Dickey, *Poems* 1957-1967, (New York, 1974), p. 243

Childhood Hills

> I tried to show two things in the poem: first, the recognition of this being that he's now a bird and no longer a man, and his realization that he can navigate by means of the stars; second, the gradual fading of his identity as a human being through this long voyage. (31)

During the bird's long voyage, he navigates by the stars, dreaming at one point that he sees the Southern Cross. Dickey takes advantage of this by having the bird reflect back to his life as a man, wherein he had believed in another Cross, which he now (as a bird) labels false. This can only be another way of Dickey reflecting his ambivalence about Christianity:

> He sees the Southern Cross
> Painfully over the horizon   drawing itself
> Together   inching
> Higher each night of the world   thorn
> Points   tilted   he watches   not to be taken in
> By the False Cross   as in
> Another life   not taken

The theme of reincarnation is one of the ways in which Dickey creates life beyond death. He must create such life because of his fear of total extinction and his inability to conceptualize heaven. The poet and critic, Richard Howard, describes this fear he finds in **Buckdancer's Choice** :

> Obsession, madness, excess: the burden
> of Buckdancer's choice is altogether

---

(31) James Dickey, *Self-Interviews,* (New York, 1970), p. 164

new in the poet, and crowned or ballasted,
by a pervasive terror of extinction. (32)

That "terror of extinction" (33) is treated well in the poem *"The Escape"* (34) from the **Buckdancer's Choice** collection. Here, Dickey speaks of the long tradition of burial in the family plot at Fairmont and then of the spontaneous (almost dreaded) secret purchase of his own grave plot at a little country graveyard in Alabama, which he had walked through on a hunting trip:

> I walked through the evergreen gates
> of the forest ranger's station,
> And out to my car, and drove
> To the county seat, and bought
> My own secret grave plot there
> For thirty-seven dollars and a half

And yet he somehow hopes not to die and shows his fear of it in the ending lines of the poem:

> I remember that, and sleep
> Easier, seeing the animal head
> Nuzzling the fragment of Scripture,
> Browsing, before the first blotting rain
> On the fragile book
> Of the new dead, on words I take care,
> Even in sleep, not to read,
> Hoping for Genesis.

---

(32) Richard Howard, *Alone with America,* (New York, 1969), p. 91
(33) Ibid., p. 91
(34) James Dickey, *Poems 1957-1967,* (New York, 1974), p. 203

Dickey is not being fully truthful when he states that "the Bible to me is a great work of literature only" (35). In his long poem *"May Day Sermon to the Women of Gilmer County, Georgia, by a Woman Preacher leaving the Baptist Church"* (36), he returns again to religion and the bible as the fabric underlying the theme of the poem. Dickey is not making a statement about the literate quality of the Bible but, rather, its religious content and about how people can use the word of God for evil and malevolent ends. Dickey, himself, has described *"May Day Sermon"* :

> *"May Day Sermon"* is about the malevolent power God has under certain circumstances; that is, when He is controlled and "interpreted" by people of malevolent tendencies. In this case God is neither more nor less than a combination of the Old Testament and a half-mad Georgia hill farmer. (37)

"Above all, the poem is an indictment of containers, restrictions, barriers—including organized religion. The father is like the vindictive God of the Old Testament" (38), writes Thomas O. Sloan. In *"May Day Sermon"*, Dickey deals with God and the devil against the backdrop of a sermon warning the girls of Gilmer County, Georgia to be wary of affairs with their lovers and relating how a girl gets beaten by her father (whom she subsequently murders) for just such an affair with her motorcycle lover. The strong images of the beating can be seen in these lines:

---

(35) James Dickey, *Self-Interviews*, (New York, 1970), p. 78
(36) James Dickey, *Poems 1957-1967*, (New York, 1974), p. 3
(37) James Dickey, *Self-Interviews*, (New York, 1970), p. 183
(38) Thomas O. Sloan, "The Open Poem is a Now Poem: Dickey's May Day Sermon", ***James Dickey: The Expansive Imagination***, (Florida, 1973), p. 96

Pat Mullan

> On the red clay floor of Hell   she screaming
>   her father screaming
>
> Scripture   CHAPter and verse   beating it
>   into her with a weeping
>
> Willow branch   the animals stomping   she
>   prancing and climbing

And these lines describe her love affair as being the work of the devil:

> Die out as her freckled flesh   as flesh and
>   the Devil twist and turn
>
> Her body to love   cram her mouth with
>   defiance   give her words
>
> To battle with the Bible's in the air: she shrieks
>   Sweet Jesus and God
>
> I'm glad   O my God—darling   O lover
>   O angel-stud   dear heart

Dickey has also stated: "I wanted to make the Bible, or a certain interpretation of the Bible which permits cruelty, the final focus of the poem." (39) When this poem was first published, its harsh religious overtones raised many protests, as evidenced by these words of Thomas O. Sloan:

> Soon after the poem first appeared in the **Atlantic** in April, 1967, a man who signed himself "the founder

---

(39) James Dickey, *Self-Interviews*, (New York, 1970), p. 184

of the Poetry Society of New Hampshire" wrote a letter to the editor insisting that the **Atlantic** apologize to the "good people of the Baptist denomination as well as to the high art of poetry." (40)

There is, therefore, overwhelming evidence throughout James Dickey's poetry supporting the fact that he is engrossed in an attempt to, on the one hand, substantiate his early Southern Christian upbringing and, on the other hand, exorcise himself from it. He has been unsuccessful in achieving neither and his confident statements to the contrary are unfounded. Perhaps these assertions and statements, to use Dickey's own words, are part of the process of inventing conditions under which he can live with himself. In fact, James Dickey should have the final say in the matter himself:

> All poetry, I suspect, is nothing more or less than an attempt to discover or invent conditions under which one can live with oneself. I have been called a mystic, a vitalist, a pantheist, an antirationalist, and a good many other things. I have not been conscious of the applicability of any of these labels, although they very well may all apply. At any rate, what I have always striven for is to find some way to incarnate my best moments—those which, in memory, are most persistent and obsessive. (41)

---

(40) Thomas O. Sloan, "The Open Poem is a Now Poem: Dickey's May Day Sermon", *James Dickey: The Expansive Imagination,* (Florida, 1973), p. 86

(41) James Dickey, *Babel to Byzantium,* (New York, 1968), p. 292

Bibliography

Davison, Peter. "The Great Grassy World from Both Sides", *James Dickey: The Expansive Imagination,* edited by Richard J. Calhoun, Florida, 1973.

Dickey, James. *Babel to Byzantium.* New York, 1968

Dickey, James. *Poems 1957-1967.* New York, 1974

Dickey, James *Self-Interviews.* New York, 1970

Gregor, Arthur. "James Dickey, American Romantic", *James Dickey: The Expansive Imagination,* edited by Richard J. Calhoun, Florida, 1973

Hill, Robert W. "James Dickey: Comic Poet", *James Dickey: The Expansive Imagination,* edited by Richard J. Calhoun, Florida, 1973

Howard, Richard. *Alone with America.* New York, 1969

Lensing, George. "James Dickey and the Movements of Imagination", *James Dickey: The Expansive Imagination,* edited by Richard J. Calhoun, Florida, 1973.

Silverstein, Norman. "James Dickey's Muscular Eschatology", *Contemporary Poetry in America,* edited by Robert Boyers, New York, 1974.

Childhood Hills

Sloan, Thomas O. *"The Open Poem is a Now Poem: Dickey's May Day Sermon"*, **James Dickey: The Expansive Imagination,** edited by Richard J. Calhoun, Florida, 1973.

And, Finally:
© Of Conscious Evil and
©*Who Killed Hammarskjold?*

Extract from the novel
© *Of Conscious Evil*

Washington, D.C.

The DJ at Xanadu wore a red beehive hairdo, false eyelashes, press-on fingernails and a big, fluffy boa draped around her neck. 'She' had always fancied Larry Sanderson but he had never been interested. It was Saturday and she spotted him at the bar.
"Larry, Honey, where have you been lately?" she gushed.
"Working, Sydney. Just working. Nothing more exotic," said Larry.
"You know what they say about that, Honey. All work and no play makes Larry a dull boy. Just let me know when you want to play. I can promise you a good time."
"Sydney, love, thanks. I think I just want to be alone tonight."

This excerpt from *Of Conscious Evil* is published with permission from Citron Press, the independent publishing house devoted to supporting new fiction.
Visit www.citronpress.co.uk

Childhood Hills

"Honey, you don't know what you're missing," said Sydney in a huff as she glided back to play some more selections before the show began.

Xanadu was an upscale gay entertainment place with a bar, restaurant and club. Larry Sanderson seldom went there. It was a bit too yuppie for him. But he enjoyed the shows. Larry managed to keep his private and public personas apart. No-one at the NSC knew he was gay. If they thought about him at all, they'd probably conclude that he was asexual, just like his computers. That suited Sanderson. The NSC was a macho heterosexual place. Coming out of the closet could only lead to trouble. There was still lingering resentment over the President's 'gays in the military' policy.

Most people were dancing. The floor was packed and there was a party atmosphere in the place. As Larry watched, spotlights shone on the three circular tables in the center of the floor, illuminating the table dancers, the stars of the evening. They were all good-looking, well-built young men wearing only the skimpiest of red silk underwear. The choreography was professional, their dancing excellent; always provocative but never lewd. Larry had seen the trio before but he never tired watching them. As he sipped his gin and tonic he couldn't help noticing the fair-haired young man looking at him intently from the other side of the bar. When he caught his eye the young man smiled. Larry looked away again. He wasn't out to pick up or be picked up.

Tonight, the bartender seemed to be auditioning. Between serving his customers he was dancing on the bar and tucking his tips suggestively down his pants. On one of his gyrations around the bar he deposited another gin and tonic in front of Larry and whispered in his ear:

"Sweetheart, this one's on Joseph," pointing to the fair-haired young man on the other side of the bar, who smiled and lifted his glass in a toast to Larry.

It must have been the numerous gin and tonics thought Larry as he fumbled to get the key into the lock on the door of his apartment. Joseph had insisted on helping him home after he had slipped off the stool at the bar in Xanadu and dazed himself when he cracked his head against the brass footrail. Now Joseph gently took the key from him and turned it in the lock. Inside Larry groped for the light switch. Again Joseph helped and as the lights came on he guided Larry over to the couch in the living room and propped him up on it with pillows.

It seemed ages later but Larry imagined he heard the door opening again, imagined he heard voices, and thought he must be dreaming. He was sure he wasn't asleep but he knew he wasn't awake either. He dreamed that hands were lifting him up in the air and carrying him. Funny how the mind can make dreams and imaginings seem so real, he thought.

He wanted to scratch the tickle on his nose but his right hand wouldn't move. He tried his left hand and it wouldn't move either. He felt panic and his struggle, as well as the smelling salts he'd just been administered, awakened him. As his eyes adjusted to the light, he could see that he was lying on his back on the bed and his wrists and ankles were tied to the bedposts. He was naked.

"Wake-up, sweetheart. Are you ready for some fun?" He knew it was Joseph. His eyes focused on the voice and he could see him standing at the foot of the bed. But there were two of him. He must be seeing double. He closed and opened his eyes but the double image didn't go away. There were two of them.

"This is my best friend, dear Larry. He wants to join in. You don't mind, do you? Two's fun but three's an orgy. Isn't that right, sweetheart?"

Larry's panic increased. He could feel his heart thumping loudly in his chest.

"Joseph, please stop. I'm not into bondage and pain. Don't do this. Let me up," he pleaded. But that just aroused chuckles in Joseph and his

Best Friend who had now emerged from the shadows with a lighted cigarillo between the fingers of his right hand.

"But my Best Friend here is into bondage and pain in a big way. Especially pain. He just loves to give it, don't you, darling?"

Best Friend said nothing. Instead he blew on the end of his cigarillo till it glowed red and then, without any warning, he stuck it into the sole of Sanderson's right foot. Sanderson's body bucked in agony on the bed but the ties held. He started to scream but Joseph stuck a face-cloth in his mouth and gagged him. Best Friend pulled away the cigarillo from Sanderson's foot and his body stopped fighting. Gradually Joseph removed the gag and Larry could smell his own burnt flesh.

"That's just an appetizer, sweetheart. Are you ready for the main course?"

" What do you want from me?" Larry wheezed. His throat hurt from the screams that were never heard.

"I'll tell you what we want, sweetheart. We want you to tell us what you're working on. We want to know what programs you're running for General Shields."

Sanderson felt as though the fire from his foot had suddenly hit his brain. They knew. Somebody had found out what he was working on. Or found out enough and had leaked it. Just as quickly he suddenly felt cold as he realized that Joseph and his Best Friend were terrorists. Maybe even the people that MacDara was looking for.

"That's not a secret. I'm working on the next version of our simulator on anti-terrorism. Everybody knows General Shields' special job in the NSC," said Larry in as controlled a voice as he could muster, still trying to talk his way out of this.

"Wrong answer, sweetheart! Best Friend doesn't like wrong answers, do you, darling?"

Knowing what was about to happen didn't help. It only made it worse. Joseph gagged him again and Best Friend stuck the glowing end of his cigarillo into Sanderson's left foot. He seemed to do it twice as long this time and when Joseph removed the gag it looked as though Sanderson was semi-conscious. Joseph stuck the smelling salts under his nose and slapped him on the cheeks till he was satisfied that Sanderson was fully alert again.

Larry Sanderson had never thought of himself as a brave person. But he'd never been tested. Until now. Now he knew he wasn't brave. He didn't want to be tortured any more. He broke down and pleaded to be set free, promised them anything if they'd spare his life. Joseph gave him some water and Larry Sanderson talked. Told them everything. Everything that he knew. About the A.I. system, about Shields, about MacDara, about the Circle of Sodom. He couldn't tell them about General Walker or Tony Thackeray because he didn't know that. But he did tell them about the investigation into Colonel McNab and the Millennium Covenant. Joseph knew when he had finished that he had told them everything. He could recognize a broken man.

"Sweetheart, you did good. You should get a prize. Don't you think so, Best Friend? Sweetheart deserves a prize, doesn't he?"

Before Sanderson knew what was happening, Joseph had gagged him again and Best Friend moved towards him from the foot of the bed. He could see the light glinting on the blade and he knew he was going to die. Somehow he didn't fight it. In those split seconds a serene calm descended on him. When his jugular was sliced open he didn't feel it. He only felt the burning in the soles of his feet. And the wetness that gushed from his throat warming his cold naked body.

Childhood Hills

Extract from the novel
©*Who Killed Hammarskjold?*

Khimki Woods,
    Moscow

    Gathering ferns was an annual Spring ritual for Sasha and Irina. Their mother cooked the fern stems, added spices, and served them as a family delicacy. The forest is central in Russian folklore and is seen as a source of food and protection. In the fall it provides mushrooms, nuts and berries and always ferns in Springtime. But the forest can be a malevolent force too. Folktales talk of the evil witch, *Baba Yaga*, and the female hobgoblins, the *kikimoras*. They punish anyone who enters the forest to do bad things.
    Sasha and Irina were so busy gathering ferns that they had lost all sense of time and direction. It was only when Sasha looked around and couldn't see Irina that she became worried. Turning back she tried to retrace her steps but the sun was beginning to set and its dying rays were penetrating the treetops. Feeling panic she called Irina's name louder and louder but there was no answer. She started to run but the forest floor was littered with obstacles. Her foot caught a root and she stumbled. Instead of trying to break her own fall she clung to her precious ferns, afraid of losing them. Pitched forward her head hit a fallen tree stunning her. Everything seemed to be getting darker and darker and she thought she might be losing consciousness. But she didn't. She lay there for a while feeling the pain in her head begin to throb. Then she got up slowly and started looking for her sister again. She walked this time, calling Irina's name over and over again. Finally she heard the

screams. Terrifying screams. Her sister's screams. Ignoring her own safety, she dropped her precious ferns and ran towards the screams.

Minutes later she saw her. Irina was standing with her back firmly against a tree, her arms behind her holding the treetrunk, looking as though she had been impaled there. Her screams had been replaced by loud sobbing. Sasha ran towards her and tried to take her in her arms, asking her over and over again what was wrong, but Irina wouldn't budge. Sasha saw the terror in her sister's eyes and turned in the direction she was staring.

She saw the dim outline of a car but nothing else. Letting go of Irina she approached the car slowly. It was an old car, a Lada. She was almost on top of the car before she saw them. Her hands automatically flew to her mouth to stifle her own screams. But she knew she had to remain in control. For her sister's sake. Slowly her mind began to comprehend what her eyes were telling her.

The woman was lying on her side with her face pressed against the window. Her eyes were open and staring, left like that when rigor mortis set in. The other side of her face was missing entirely. Just a bloody pulp with one eyeball dangling where her cheekbone should have been. Bits of flesh and clotted blood had pebbledashed the inside of the windscreen. The man was sitting upright, too upright, behind the steering wheel. A shotgun was braced between his knees, the muzzle in his mouth, and his finger wrapped around the trigger. His brains were sprayed all over the car.

The official news release buried in small print in the Moscow Daily News simply stated that Leonid Fomin and his wife had ended their life in a murder suicide pact brought on by the husband's gambling debts and their mutual descent into alcoholism and despair.

Childhood Hills

Shannon,
Ireland.

'The Green Ireland of your Ancestors'
Dr. Ernesto 'Che' Guevara Lynch

Aeroflot Flight 697 landed at 2:30 pm, just fifteeen minutes later than scheduled. Conor Brady grabbed his carryon bag and was one of the first off the plane. His Irish passport propelled him through and soon he was turning the keys in his rented car. Conor was no stranger to Ireland. This was his fourth visit since he had left Argentina. His trips to Ireland had been necessary. Necessary for his own soul; necessary for his own identity; necessary for his understanding of his grandfather; necessary to help him survive under a false name. It was the 'green Ireland of his ancestors'. Those words had branded his soul ever since the day he saw the postcard that Che Guevara had sent to his father from Dublin in 1964. His mind's eye still saw the words *'I am in the green Ireland of your ancestors. When the television found out they came to ask me about the genealogy of the Lynches'.*

But he wasn't thinking about any of this as he maneuvered the car through Shannon and headed for Ennis and Galway. He was thinking instead about Owen MacDara. He was troubled by his mission this time. Usually he never gave these assignments a second thought. Always the target was nothing more than a target. A cardboard cutout. Maybe it was MacDara's Irishness that bothered him. No, he thought about that for a minute. He had no compunction about taking out an Argentinian. Why should it be any different with an Irishman? Maybe it was curiosity? Maybe it was the need to know the victim? Maybe he was losing it? Whatever it was, something inside him made him want to meet MacDara, made him want to see what made MacDara tick. Maybe it was the need to find a victim worthy of his skills. Maybe he wanted to risk himself this time. Maybe it was boredom. He had briefed himself well on Owen MacDara: born in Ireland, paramedic in the US Army in Korea, black belt in Karate, founder of his own consulting company, self-made millionaire, special agent for the President of the United States, lost his pregnant Kate only a year ago, and now the biggest obstacle for Misha. Yes, he had to meet MacDara.

Conor was still trying to come to grips with this behavior of his when he realized that the city of Galway was behind him and he was squeezing his car through the crowded narrow streets of Oughterard, the village beside Lough Corrib. He pulled the car over, stopped and ran in to Keogh's, the little village supermarket, to satisfy his addiction for a Coke. His non-alcoholic beverage of choice. As he paid for it the mounted photo of Bob Hope taken on his last visit was proudly displayed over the cash register. To Conor's curious look, the lady at the register said;

"Ah, sure he's just a darlin' man. Comes here all the time. To visit his daughter, you know. She's been livin' here for years."

As Conor slid the coke into the slot beside the ashtray and slipped the car into first gear he thought that the little scene involving Bob Hope's picture defined the Ireland that he'd come to know. A place where everybody knew everybody. Small enough for the famous and the notorious to rub shoulders in the nearest pub with the locals. A place where nobody was unduly impressed by celebrity. A place where people respected your privacy. A good place for a Conor Brady.

A few minutes later the landscape changed dramatically. The green fields were gone. Replaced by brown heather dotted with clumps of yellow gorse running down to shimmering water sparkling like diamonds. And bogland reaching the foothills on the horizon with the hazy outline of the Maamturk Mountains tracing craggy lines in the sky. He was now in Connemara. Forty-five minutes later he reached Clifden, the capital of Connemara, a small market town on the Atlantic shore. He was expected at the Abbeyglen Castle Hotel. He had stayed here before. They made a point of remembering.

Childhood Hills

Owen MacDara lay on his back about a half mile from Ardree House. His elbows dug into a bed of springy sphagnum moss and he watched a large black bird circle overhead. Soon it was joined by a smaller bird and they climbed higher, two black dots against the blue ceiling. Flying free. That's what Kate and my son are doing now. Their souls are flying free. But I'm not a believer. I don't believe in reincarnation. Still? He pondered deeply as he watched the two birds separate. Now only one remained. The little one. A tiny black speck in that vast expanse of blue. Suddenly, he was twelve years old again, lying out on his father's bog, resting from his morning's turf cutting, watching the lark in the sky above. I wrote a poem about that. I wonder if I can still remember the words. Let me see….

The barking dog brought him out of it. He pressed his hands deep into the moss till he felt firmer ground. Then he leveraged himself to his feet and looked across the hillside. A farmer was herding his sheep, his dog rounding up the strays. It was time to go. He'd flown in from Moscow two days ago and had spent the time tracking down Major Lacey. It hadn't really been very difficult. That's the advantage of Ireland. Small enough that everyone knows everyone else. Or have a sense that they do. One phone call to a friend, a member of the Military History Society of Ireland and he soon discovered that the Major was in reality Richard de Lacey, the seventh Earl and head of the de Laceys. It was no secret that Lacey had been a mercenary with 'Mad Mike' Hoare in the Congo. Colonel O'Beirne of the Military History Society seemed to take a vicarious pleasure in that when he briefed MacDara. President Mobutu of Zaire employed Hoare in the Congo in the early sixties. Some of the actions of Lacey and his mercenary colleagues, such as rescuing nuns, made heroes of them. But they were totally ruthless. They took no prisoners, especially their Simba rebel captives. O'Beirne was only too glad to relay stories of these events to MacDara. Especially if it included dinner and copious amounts of his favorite South African pinotage. They were on their second bottle. Actually the Colonel was on their second bottle and MacDara was still on his second glass when the stories started to flow.

"Y'know, Owen", said Colonel O'Beirne, using 'Owen' in that instant intimacy bestowed by alcohol, "this is confidential. Not classified. Not secret, mind you. But, still confidential. Right from the horse's mouth. In Jo'burg."

"Jo'burg?", quizzed MacDara.

"Johannesburg. I was attached to the UN in the seventies and eighties. Ireland, neutral nation and all that. Thought we could be honest brokers between the ANC and the Afrikaners. It was O'Brien's influence, y'know. The Cruiser."

"The Cruiser?", Owen repeated, although he already knew the reference.

"Sure. The Cruiser. Conor Cruise O'Brien. Another relic of the Congo. He was the UN Representative in the Congo in 1961. You knew that, didn't you?"

"Yes, yes. Of course," said MacDara, but the Colonel had moved on, not really waiting for an answer.

"Where was I? Jo'burg?", continued the Colonel, finishing his glass and refilling it. He offered to top up Owen's glass but Owen declined.

"Kruger. That's who told me. He had been there with Lacey. In the Congo. When Mike Hoare formed '4 Commando'. He was never sure of Lacey's standing in the chain of command. As a Major Lacey was a rank higher than Hoare's rank of Captain."

The Colonel stopped just long enough to gulp down more of the pinotage and then looked intimately at MacDara, "Did you know that about a third of '4 Commando' were South Africans?"

"No, I didn't. Why so many?", asked Owen.

"That's easy! South Africa were up to their ears in the Congo."

Major Lacey was still alive and living only a few miles away. Owen had called that morning and made an appointment. The Major was expecting him at three. He glanced at his watch. Just past noontime.

Childhood Hills

Conor Brady had also heard the dog barking. He adjusted the right eyepiece of his Nikons and watched the skill of the sheepdog for thirty seconds. For the past hour he'd lain on a rocky, heathery knoll that commanded a view of Ardree House and the surrounding countryside and watched Owen MacDara lying on his back staring at the sky. If only binoculars had the ability to read minds. He'd have given a lot to know what was going through MacDara's head as he lay there staring at the sky, occasionally flicking a hand across his face. A perfect target. I could easily fill my contract right here. Getting away couldn't be easier. There isn't a soul around except for that farmer and his sheepdog. But I'm in no hurry. MacDara has a flight booked to New York three days from now. New York will do fine. He swung the binoculars back in time to see MacDara rise to his feet and walk back towards Ardree House, picking his way through the hidden minefield of bogland swamp. He was beginning to enjoy his cat and mouse game with MacDara. Usually these contracts of Misha's were boring and predicable. Not this time. He was in no hurry to take out MacDara. He put the binoculars back in their case, slung them over his shoulder and began his trek back down to the main road.

MacDara was only six miles from Ardree House on a road that he had travelled numerous times. And, yet he couldn't find the major's house. He turned back for the third time, traversing the same stretch of roadway. This time he saw it. The opening was barely visible between overgrown hedgerows and whin bushes. It had to be the entrance, he decided as the bushes brushed the side windows of his car. Once inside he could see that he was on a solid lane, much wider than he expected. It was covered with tufts of grass and weeds, testimony to its lack of use. A jungle of trees lined each side, blocking any vision of what lay beyond. So it was a surprise when he turned a corner to find himself in front of a house that had once been an elegant mansion. The architecture was mixed, part French chateau with Palladian style wings, but it had been allowed to deteriorate. An ornate fountain, now dry and surrounded by ferns and nettles, formed a centerpiece in the middle ground that used to be a circular driveway. As MacDara left his car and walked toward the front door he could imagine other days, days of dinner parties and carriages arriving with ladies and gentlemen in their finery.

MacDara was expected but not at the front door. A door in the right wing was ajar and Major Richard de Lacey, a tall thin, Patrician looking man in his early seventies, extended a bony hand with a remarkably firm grip.

"Mr. MacDara?"

"Please just call me Owen. And thank you for taking the time to see me."

"Do call me Richard. All the 'blow-ins' call me Major but the locals always refer to me as 'His Lordship' although I have never used that ridiculous title. And, Owen, don't thank me. Time is all I have these days. Now, just follow me. Mind your step here. The floor is a bit irregular at this corner."

They negotiated a narrow, dimly-lit corridor whose walls were covered with ancestral paintings, dark in pigment, many of them almost floor to ceiling, until they emerged into a flagstoned entrance hall squared between two enormous fireplaces. MacDara had a glimpse of pistols on the mantlepiece and crossed sabres on the wall as the Major's loping gait seemed to gather speed crossing the hall. Almost in a tour guide voice, without stopping or turning around, the Major said, over his shoulder:

"We haven't used this entrance in years. Not since our grandmother passed away."

Crossing into another corridor extending beyond the central entrance hall they soon reached a large dark green oak door. The Major opened it and ushered MacDara inside. The contrast was stark. Comfortable chairs, booklined walls, collectables and art, all warmed by a blazing fire in the hearth made the room personal, lived-in, human.

"Please make yourself comfortable", said the Major, directing Owen to a chair by the fire as he crossed the room to an array of drinks displayed on a corner table.

"Cognac, Irish, Scotch?"

" A Paddy please, if you have it."

"Indeed I do. I like it myself. Smooth. I'll join you."

The Major returned with two large Waterford tumblers generously filled with the amber glow of Paddy. They toasted in the Gaelic.

"Slainte!"

The Major didn't sit down. Instead he wandered over to the bookshelves. He looked as though he intended to reach for a volume, then changed his mind and turned to face MacDara.

"The original De Lacey came to Ireland in the twelfth century with Strongbow. The Norman Invasion! And you know that Strongbow was Richard de Clare, the Earl of Pembroke, a Norman himself. So when the Irish say that the English invaded Ireland , it was really the Normans, my ancestors. A century or two later we'd become 'more Irish than the Irish themselves'. But you know all that, don't you, Owen?"

"Yes, Richard," said Owen and quickly tried to keep the Major from wandering, "the reason I came to see you…"

"I know the reason you came to see me," said the Major and then proceeded as though that was unimportant.

"How many of us own our ancestral lands today?" It was a rhetorical question. He didn't wait for an answer.

"Very few. But we still do. It hasn't been easy. How much do you think it would cost to heat this whole place? The Colonial Service of the Crown. That's how we did it. That's how we kept our lands. We practiced the Art of War and the spoils of those foreign wars paid our servants and our debts. But the Empire ended and we weren't needed."

"And the Congo…..?", MacDara tried again.

"What skills did I have. Only those of the warrior. It was either that or lose our lands. Can you see me in some one roomed cottage? Of course you can't. So I fought for the person who paid me the most. Colonel Mike Hoare was a fellow Irishman. He and I served together in the British army. So when he asked me to join him I couldn't refuse."

"But the CIA and MI5…And the KGB?," asked MacDara.

"Oh, don't be so naïve, Owen. I worked for all of them. Numerous times. War is a dirty business!"

"But why the Secretary General of the UN?", MacDara's tone got louder.

"The UN! Hah! They were not peacekeepers. They were up to their eyeballs in that mess in the Congo. The Secretary General was one of their Field Commanders. He was fair game and we weren't playing by the Marquis of Queensbury rules. Besides Colonel Mike could never have paid me what the Yanks and the Russians did. You see, Owen, I would have done anything to save our lands. I did not want to be remembered as the de Lacey who lost the ancestral home and sold off the family titles to some vulgar Texas oil millionaire."

He gulped down his Paddy, refilled his glass and offered Owen another. But Owen declined and went straight to the heart of the matter, his reason for being there.

"Richard, we know from the KGB documents that Zhukov was the Russian who contracted you for the Congo assignment but they didn't give the American's name. Zhukov is dead so he can't tell us. That's why I am here."

"You know, old boy, you really can't prove any of this and I've got little time left so it doesn't matter to me any more. Prostate cancer. Six months at best", said the Major matter of factly, as he finally conceded that his strength had ebbed and sank into the armchair opposite MacDara. Owen waited, sensing that he would get what he came for.

"I never liked the American. A bully, I'd say. It doesn't matter to me if you know his name or not. It was Kearns. Yes, that was it. I don't believe I ever knew his first name. We weren't really on a first name basis. But I don't see what good it will do you. It was obvious to me that they were just somebody's messenger boys. And you may not want to find out who that somebody was. For your own health, I mean."

The Major was enjoying the company and would have been quite happy to entertain MacDara all evening. But Owen had got what he came for and, as graciously as he could, made his exit. As he turned at the green oak door to say goodbye, the Major spoke again, his voice tinged with just the right sense of curiosity and bemusement.

"Owen, I do think you people should talk with each other. I told all of this to that young Russian lady from the UN who came to see me a couple of days ago. What was her name? Anna? Nina? Something like that."

Deep River,
Connecticut.

General Bartley Shields was at his house in Deep River, Connecticut, when he got the call from CIA Director Richard Smallwood.

Smallwood was in New York on company business so it was easy to take the Amtrak train to Essex, a small sleepy town on the Connecticut river, about a twenty minute drive from Shields' house. As he descended from the train, dragging his carryon bag behind him, he didn't recognize the General standing on the other side of the railroad tracks, wearing jeans that were threadbare at the knees and a misshapen Aran sweater that had seen better days.

Bart Shields took his hands out of his pockets, waved a greeting and waited as Dick Smallwood crossed the tracks. A few minutes later they were headed out of Essex in Shields' ten year old Mercedes.

The General's house was deceptive. At first glance it appeared to be a single story ranch but that was only the 'tip of the iceberg'. Once inside the house revealed its secret: three stories clung to the hillside and a second story deck captured the panorama of the Connecticut river and the lush surrounding countryside. The evening was warm and the sky a clear blue, perfect for the table that awaited them out on the deck. Dick Smallwood was a vegetarian and Millie Shields, renowned among the Washington wives for her skill in the kitchen, had prepared a vegetarian goulash with wild rice followed by her special dessert of pears in red wine sauce. Bart already had a bottle of good chablis cooling on ice and proceeded to decant a bottle of Cousino Macoul, his favorite Chilean red.

Listening to Dick Smallwood's superlatives about the 'best vegetarian goulash he'd ever had' and watching her husband circumcise a fresh macanudo cigar, Millie knew it was time to make her exit.

Bart Shields reached for the tall black bottle of Otard VSOP and poured two generous glasses of cognac. They both sipped and savored in silence, lulled into a feeling of wellbeing by Millie's marvellous meal, the excellent cognac and the peaceful vista that stretched beneath them to the horizon. Bart Shields finally broke the silence.

"Dick, I gather you've got something important to tell me."

"That's right, Bart," replied Dick Smallwood as he reached into the inner pocket of his jacket and retrieved a small, black, scuffed and dog-eared notebook. Handing it across the table, he said:

"Read the first three pages."

Bart Shields opened the notebook and, looking at the small dense writing, fished his reading glasses from his breast pocket. It seemed obvious that the writer had wanted to cram as much as possible into the notebook. He read the first page:

This is my insurance policy, life insurance to be exact, and I hope that it never needs to be used. On the other hand, maybe this story can be told when I am dead—to set the record straight, to correct the falsehoods of history. I haven't decided that yet. For now, its only purpose is to keep me alive. This notebook will be made public if I meet an untimely end. Everything recorded here is true. This I swear by Almighty God.

Signed this 5th day of October, 1969,
John Casey Wainwright.

Childhood Hills

The next two pages were written in the same dense style so it took Shields' full concentration. His cognac sat untouched and the ashes on his cigar had outgrown the ashtray and toppled onto the table. But he was oblivious to all of that. Snatches of Wainwright's 'insurance policy' seared themselves into his brain:

'I was there when Director Dulles ordered the assassination of Patrice Lumumba'…'we were protecting the billions we had invested in the Congo's mineral resources'…'Helms has detroyed all the documents'… 'my words written here will be all that survive'… 'it was the decision to take out Dag Hammarskjold that has destroyed me'…' Washington and Moscow are in collusion'….

Shields read the last paragraph at the bottom of page three before closing the notebook and looking across at Dick Smallwood: *'on the following pages I have recorded the key events and decisions covering CIA involvement in Africa. The dates and locations of each event are accurate. I have identified the people who participated, including those who made the decisions and gave the orders. Where I was present I have admitted that. Where I was culpable I have said so. I am not using this to exonerate myself.'*

"Wainwright! Didn't he disappear from the face of the earth? Just like Judge Crater!," asked Shields, rhetorically.

"Yes! He disappeared alright. About a year after he wrote this. He left the company and just dropped out of sight. It was news for a couple of weeks until it was pushed off the page," replied Smallwood.

"Rumor had it that he was in the running for Director once upon a time," said Shields, seeking confirmation of his recollection.

" I believe if the timing had been right for the appointment of a Director from within the company, he'd have made it. Jack Wainwright had the inside track," confirmed Smallwood.

"How did you get this notebook? And what happened to him?" asked Bart Shields.

"I'll take your last question first, Bart," said Dick Smallwood, as Shields reached over and refilled his cognac glass, pushing aside a weak protest. "Around the time Wainwright was writing this he was also getting ill. Severe allergic reactions. Heart palpitations. Rashes. Lupus."

"Lupus! I thought that was a woman's disease," interjected Shields.

"That's what I thought too, Bart. So I've educated myself on the subject. Apparently a small percentage of men also suffer from the disease. There's basically two forms of it, systemic and drug induced. Some people have gotten lupus from medication, especially drugs that are used to control heart arrhythmia. Nobody seems to know what causes systemic lupus. There was no agreement in Wainwright's case and he had not been on any heart medicine. Some people believed that his ailments were stress related. Others, less kind, said that it was all in his mind, that it was psychological, self-induced. At any rate, he got worse and worse until he couldn't work any more. This was all kept quiet by the company, of course."

"What happened to him?"

"Well, he was finally diagnosed with something called MCS, although most of the medical profession will not acknowledge that there is such a disease."

"What's MCS?"

"Multiple chemical sensitivities. Wainwright had developed severe allergic and immune system reaction to anything and everything that was remotely chemical. And, in our modern world, that means practically everything."

Smallwood was caught up in the drama of his story and Shields noted that he had barely touched the last cognac he'd given him. Getting up from the table he stretched himself, looked out over the Connecticut river in the far distance, and then turned towards Shields.

"But we think he may still be alive although no one, not even his family, has heard from him in at least ten years. He quit the agency, left everything and everyone and went in search of a place that was free from the poisons that were killing him. He has one daughter and she last heard from him ten years ago. From Fort Davis, Texas."

"Fort Davis? That's as far west in Texas as you can get?"

"It sure is!," said Smallwood, sitting down again and taking a sip of his cognac.

"Now to answer your first question. I'm afraid we got his notebook by devious means. We discovered that he had instructed his daughter to turn it over to the Washington Post after his death. The rest was simple. We faked a death certificate and convinced her that he was dead. Then we waited. About a week later she called the Washington Post. She didn't know that we were intercepting her calls. So it was easy to set up a 'sting' operation and pose as the Washington Post. She had no reason to suspect anything so she turned over the notebook to us."

There was the suggestion of a smile on Smallwood's face, more like the look of satisfaction on the face of a cat that had just swallowed a mouse. Shields exclaimed.

"Jeez, Dick! You don't give a shit about the laws of the land, do you?"

Smallwood didn't answer that. Shields picked up Wainwright's notebook again, opened it and said, softly, almost to himself:

"There's one thing that I must know. Who ordered the assassination of Dag Hammarskjold?"

He paged through the notebook, almost reluctant to find the answer. When he did he read it without breathing, then he sank deeper into his chair deflating like a large balloon that has just burst. Smallwood looked at him.

"Now you know why I had to see you here. Away from Washington."

"Who else knows this?" asked Shields.

"Only you and I. And Wainwright. If he's still alive," Smallwood replied.

"Well, if he is alive he may not stay alive much longer. We'd better find him fast. I suggest we get MacDara on this immediately."

"I agree. Where is he?"

"He and Leslie Scott are in New York. Nyack. They went to talk to Kearns."

About the author

Pat Mullan, a native of Derry, Ireland, has lived in England, Canada and the USA. He spent two years with the US Army in Japan and Korea. Formerly a banker, he is a graduate of Northwestern University and the State University of New York where he studied creative writing.

He lives in Connemara, in the west of Ireland, with his Scottish wife Jean and their two young daughters. His novel, *Of Conscious Evil,* will be available soon on *Amazon.co.uk*. He is currently at work on a new novel, *Who Killed Hammarskjold?*

Stay in Touch with Pat Mullan on the Internet

Pat Mullan's website: ~~www.Athryhouse.com~~ *www.patmullan.com* is under construction as this work goes to publication. Pat invites you to visit there from time to time. New poetry, new art and new writings will be available at the site. You will also find out where to buy his novels. *Of Conscious Evil* will be available soon on Amazon.co.uk. He plans to complete *Who Killed Hammarskjold?* within the next six months and the website will keep you informed about its progress from manuscript to published novel.

Some of Pat Mullan's work has been published on the internet e-zines of the Dublin Writers Workshop; you can find him in a few of their *Acorn* e-zines at *www.dublinwriters.org* . You can also find him at another Irish literary site: *www.scriobh.com*

Pat welcomes correspondence from his readers. You can e-mail him at *mullan@iol.ie*

Printed in the United Kingdom
by Lightning Source UK Ltd.
362